Embrace

عِناق

Najwan Darwish

Embrace

عِناق

Translated from Arabic by
Atef Alshaer with Paul Batchelor

poetry
translation
centre

First published in 2020
by the Poetry Translation Centre Ltd
The Albany, Douglas Way, London, SE8 4AG

www.poetrytranslation.org

ISBN: 978-1-9161141-2-8

A catalogue record for this book is available from the British Library

Typeset in Minion / Sakkal Majalla
by Poetry Translation Centre Ltd / WorldAccent

Series Editor: Edward Doegar
Cover Design: Kit Humphrey
Printed in the UK by T.J. Books Limited

This book has been selected to receive financial assistance from
English PEN's PEN Translates programme, supported by Arts Council
England. English PEN exists to promote literature and our understanding
of it, to uphold writers' freedoms around the world, to campaign against
the persecution and imprisonment of writers for stating their views, and to
promote the friendly co-operation of writers and the free exchange of ideas.
www.englishpen.org

The PTC is supported using public funding by
Arts Council England

Contents

Introduction

A time without writing	أَدْهُرٌ بِلا كِتابة
a silent wolf	ذئبةٌ صامِتة
on the path of ships.	على طَريقِ القَوافِل.

In 'A time without writing…', a short poem quoted above in its entirety, Najwan Darwish creates a characteristically compelling and yet inexplicable image. It feels at once immediate, honest and somehow incongruous. This unparaphrasable quality is at the heart of what makes Darwish so fascinating as a poet and yet so difficult to write about. Even so, his style does stand out: he is unhesitant in his voice; his impressions are chiseled by fact and emotion. There is courage to the acute insight of his poetry. It is often pessimistic, summoning up melancholia from the depth of unfathomable experiences and from the human condition itself. What makes Darwish particularly impressive is his control in doing so; his poems never veer off topic, never meander into the prosaic forest. He manages to speak in concrete terms about existential experience in startlingly new ways.

Born in Jerusalem to a Palestinian family, Darwish grew up living among, and educating himself about, a wide variety of religious and literary traditions, the living heritage of the city. This took in the Christian and Islamic traditions as well as ancient and modern literary approaches. Darwish has also travelled widely, engaging and deepening his understanding of symbols and meanings from different cultures. All these are deployed in his poems in ways that lend his poetry historic resonance, but also modern energy. The confluence of cultures and traditions give rise to startling insight as well as contradictions. These are reconciled through irony and, ultimately, love of and commitment to these traditions as *living materials* subject to revision and refinement. Darwish's poetry both expresses and transcends the Palestinian condition.

Naturally, the historical injustices visited upon Palestine are often evoked in his poems. His poems often articulate a collective grief. This is the grief of occupied Palestinians, whose historical consideration is made ever more difficult by Israel's incessant barbarity towards them. It is utterly distressing that the so-called 'international community' supports Israel by using its demeaning terms and references to frame the Palestinians as nameless, stateless and without history. Darwish conjures up the depth of his people's history in the face of this colonial machination and denial. Inevitably, this political background is present in Darwish's poetry, but never in didactic or polemic ways. It is embedded in the human situations which give rise to these individual expressions of the lyric, often in the form of a lament for the deep injustice and oppression of occupation and imperialism. Poetry speaks through silences present in places and visible in the enduring habits and living memories.

Darwish makes this grief singularly poignant. His poetic voice emanates from personal insight into the state of Palestine, a state that is deteriorating apace and offers no concrete hope for the future. Yet, the Palestine he projects in his verse is also a metaphor. Darwish is riddled with existential angst, and his lucid gift of rendering pain audible is deployed sharply to make the existential unbearably present in verse. Dangerous colonial politics, history and personal impressions make up the human drama which the poet presents and protests against at the same time.

In much of Arabic poetry, there are glimmers of hope, but here sorrow dominates. Although quiet, ironic at times, controlled and competent, Darwish's poetry is steeped in history and cultural allusions without being overwrought. He registers, commemorates and celebrates ordinary encounters, places, figures and situations, rendering their humanity present and meaningful. The concision and directness of his verse, with twists and turns often captured in lucid images, make his poetry particularly amenable to translation. The concreteness of his poetic voice lends itself to transferable images and constructs across many languages, and certainly in English.

Here there is a search for tacit wisdom through poetry in a world ever hobbled, cynical and unstable. Language is not quite what it seems in Darwish's verse. This makes the act of translation challenging, yet rewarding, in that stable meanings are not readily there for the translation to lean on. Instead, the translator is called upon to translate voice and sense, rather than meaning in the immediate sense. This is connected to Darwish's gift which lies in his astute ability to transcend national and ideological givens in pursuit of poetic aesthetics in a world saturated in clichés. It is not common to come across a poet so confident of his own voice with all its marvels and quirkiness within a space crowded with rhetorical flourishes.

Darwish is shrewdly aware of history and of poetic currents. But he uses these to sustain a voice of his own. This is no small feat. Darwish is not overly prolific but, when he does write, his writing counts. It stands out. It is moving and reassuring to read Darwish's poetry – this wandering poet – and find that he constructs a verse of reflective and somber mastery, a poetry close to one's own encounter with solid realities, whether political, historical, intellectual or psychological.

Atef Alshaer

Poems

تنويع على بيت للمَعَرّي

جَسَدي زُرْقةٌ نَسِيَتْها السَّماواتُ
وبُستانٌ فَرَّ مِنَ الرَّبيع
يا «خائطَ العَوالِم»
ما ضَرَّكَ لَوْ لَمْ تَخِطْني؟

Variation on a Line by al-Ma'arri

My body is a blue the sky has long forgotten;
my body is a garden lost to the spring.
You, 'tailor of the universe',
what would be lost by not sewing me?

أمام كنيسة في مستوطَنة أنْتِغوا

فَلّاحَةٌ فلسطينيّة ثَكِلَتْ إلهاً
حَمَلَتِ النّورَ والظُّلْمَةَ إلى بلاد المايا والأَزْتِك
مُنْذُ أَلْفَي سَنة وهُمْ يَمْنَعونَ تِمْثالَها مِنَ الكَلام
يَمْنَعونَها مِنْ أَنْ تَقولَ قِصَّتَها
فَلّاحَةٌ فلسطينيّة صغيرة
ثَكِلَتْ إلهاً وتَغَرَّبَتْ
مُنْذُ أَلْفَي سَنة وهيَ مُقيَّدةٌ بالحَجَرِ والطّين
سَجينةٌ تَماثيلِها الصّامتة
لا تَتَكَلَّمُ التي ثَكِلَتْ إلهاً إلّا حينَ يَصِلُ زائرٌ مِنْ قَرْيَتِها
يَحْمِلُ قَناني الزّيْت وطَحينَ اللُّجوء،
عِنَباً ذابِلاً مِنَ الخَليلِ
وشِباكاً مُمَزَّقةً مِنْ بَحْرِ الجَليل

فَلّاحَةٌ ثَكْلى
تَنْزِلُ مِنْ تِمْثالِها وتَمْسَحُ دُموعَ الزّائر.

14

In Front of a Church in the Settlement of Antigua

A Palestinian peasant girl mourned a God —
she carried light and darkness
to the country of the Maya and Aztecs
for two thousand years they have banned her statue from speaking
and prohibited her from telling her story.
A young Palestinian peasant girl
mourned a God and was exiled
for two thousand years, tied to stones and mud;
imprisoned in her silent statue
she does not talk, the one who mourned a God,
except when a visitor from her village arrives
carrying olive oil, withered grapes
from Hebron, the flour of refugees,
and torn nets from the Sea of Galilee.

A bereaved peasant girl
steps down from her statue
to wipe away the visitor's tears.

عِناق

مُرْتَبِكٌ ومُبَلَّلٌ
يَدي تَمَزَّقَتْ وهِيَ تُحاوِلُ مُعانَقَةَ جِبالٍ ووديانٍ وسُهول
والبَحْرُ الذي أَحْبَبْتُهُ أَغْرَقَني مِراراً
وما كانَ جَسَدَ العاشِقِ صارَ جُثَّةً
تَطفو على المِياه

مُرْتَبِكٌ ومُبَلَّلٌ
جُثَّتي هيَ الأُخرى
تَمُدُّ ذِراعَها
مُسْتَميتَةً
لِعِناقِ البَحْرِ الذي أَغْرَقَها.

16

Embrace

Confused, wet through,
my hands, torn reaching to embrace mountains
valleys and plains
and the sea that I loved, that drowned me over and over.
The body of the lover has become a corpse
afloat on the water.

Confused, wet through,
my corpse also stretches out its arms,
clutching, to embrace the sea that drowns it.

في مهرجانٍ شِعريّ

أَمامَ كُلِّ شاعرٍ اسمُ بِلادِهِ
ولَمْ يَكُنْ وَراءَ اسمي سِوى Jerusalem

كَمْ هُوَ مُرعِبٌ اسمُكِ يا بِلادي الصَّغيرة
التي لَمْ يَبْقَ لي سِوى اسمها
أنامُ فيه وأَسْتَيْقِظُ
اسمها الذي مِثلَ سَفينةٍ لا أَمَلَ لها بالوُصول
ولا بالرُّجوع...

لا تَصِلُ ولا تَرْجِع
لا تَصِلُ ولا تَغْرَق.

At a Poetry Festival

In front of each poet, their country's name.
Next to my name, nothing but 'Jerusalem'.

How frightening your name must be, my little country —
nothing remains of you but the name.
I sleep and I wake with it,
your name like a boat with no hope of arrival or return.

It neither arrives nor returns.
It neither arrives nor drowns.

كلام إلى وادي الصَّلِيب

لا أنتَ صَدَّقْتَ أَنِّي كَبُرْت
ولا أنا أُصَدِّقُ أَنَّكَ هُجِرْت

أَيُصَدِّقُ المَرْءُ
أنَّ يَدَيهِ ووَجهَهُ
أصبَحا خَرائبَ مَعروضةً لِلبَيع؟

يا وادِيَ ظِلِّ المَوْت
وظِلِّ الحَياة
ظِلالُنا تَتَكسَّرُ وتَتَجَمَّعُ على شُرُفاتِ بيوتِك
سَنَظَلُّ نَتَواعَدُ ونَتَوادَعُ
مِثْلَ مَوْجَتَينِ ضائعَتَينِ في بَحْرِنا الكَبير.

To the Valley of the Cross

You couldn't believe how much I'd grown;
I couldn't believe how deserted you were.

Who could believe
that his own hands and face
have become ruins put up for sale?

O valley of the shadow of death
and the shadow of life —
our shadows break and gather on the balconies of your houses.
We will keep meeting and bidding farewell
like two lost waves in a vast sea.

كلام عند مدخل القدس

يا سيِّدي، أنا، رسولُ الله قَيَّدَني بين القُدسِ ومَكَّةَ
لا أَسْتَطيعُ أَنْ أَبْرَحَ الفَضاءَ الذي بَيْنَهُما.
إنَّني أَنْتَظِرُه
وإنَّ أرْضاً لا يَهْبِطُ البُراقُ فيها لَسْتُ بِساكِنِها...
لكِنّي في بَعْضِ كَوابيسي
أَرى غُزاةً يُعَقِّمونَ مُعْجَمَ البُلدان مِنْ لُغَةِ العَرَب
أَراها وقَدَ صارت كُلُها «شِعْبَ بَوانٍ»
حَيْثُ «الفَتى العَرَبيُّ فيها غَريبُ اليَدِ والوَجْهِ...» كما تَعْرِف
فأَسْتَيْقِظُ وأنا أَرْتَجِف وأقولُ لنَفْسي:
لا تَبْقَيْ في أَرْضٍ يُقْطَعُ فيها لِسانُ العَرَب
لا تبقيْ في أَرْضٍ تُمْسَحُ فيها لُغَتُهُم
عَنْ شَواهِدِ قُبُورِهِم

ثُمَّ ما مكَّةُ والقُدْس مِنْ دونِ لُغَتِهِم؟

Words at the Gate of Jerusalem

My Lord, the Prophet chained me between Jerusalem and Mecca:
I cannot leave the space between them.
I am waiting for him,
a land that the Prophet's Burāq has not touched
is not worth living in.
But in my nightmares
I see invaders cleanse the Dictionary of Countries from the
    Arabs' language.
I see the land, the language, becoming an exile,
as Al-Mutanabbī said of the free Arab: 'a stranger in face,
    hand, and tongue'.
I wake up trembling, and say to myself
do not stay on land where the tongue of Arabs is cut,
do not stay on land where their language is erased
from their tombstones —

For what are Mecca and Jerusalem without their language?

أيّام الجحيم

لَمْ يَكُنْ بِمُسْتَطاعِنا – ونَحْنُ في الجَحيم – أَنْ نَقولَ إِنَّنا في الجَحيم
وكانَ هذا أَفْظَعَ ما في الأَمْر.

حَتَّى الآن
هذا الاعْتِرافُ المُتأخِّر
يَبْدو
بِلا مَعْنى.

The Days of Hell

We were not able — while in Hell — to say 'This is Hell.'
That was the worst thing about it.

Even today
this late admission
is meaningless.

في زنزانة الطّبيعة

أَيْنَ يَذْهَبُ إِنْسَانٌ مِنْ وَجْهِ المَوْت
المَوْتُ هوَ البَحْرُ والجَبَلُ والنَّسيم
يَتَبَرْعَمُ في مَقْطوعَةِ الحُبّ
ويَتَكَلَّلُ في كُلِّ زَفافٍ تَرْعاهُ الفُصول

أَيْنَ يُمْكِنُ أَنْ يَذْهَبَ مَوْتٌ مِنْ وَجْهِ الإِنسان
الإِنسانُ هوَ البَحْرُ والجَبَلُ والنَّسيم
يَتَبَرْعَمُ في مَقْطوعة الحُبّ
ويَتَكَلَّلُ في كُلِّ زَفافٍ تَرْعاهُ الفُصول

في زِنْزانَةِ الطَّبيعَة
يَتَجاوران، وعَنْوةً يَتَصاحَبان:
مَوْتٌ وإنسان.

In the Cell of Nature

Where should one turn from the face of death?
Death is the sea, the mountain and the breeze.
It blooms in every love song,
crowns each wedding in its season.

Where can death turn from the face of man?
Man is the sea, the mountain and the breeze.
He blooms in every love song,
crowns each wedding in its season.

In the cell of nature
they are neighbours, they are
companionable: death and man.

اهْرُب

وأسمعُ صوتاً يقول لي: اهْرُب
واترُك جزيرةَ الإنكليز وراءك
لا شيء تنتمي إليه سوى هذا المِذياع المُقَلَّدِ بإتقان
سوى سَخَّان القهوة
سوى أشجارِ الحديقة المُخطَّطة على حريرِ السماء
وأسمعُ الصّوتَ بِلغاتٍ أعرفها وأُخرى أجهَلُها:
اهْرُب
واترُك وراءك الباصات الحمراء المُتهالكة
سِكَكَ القطارات الصدئة
هذه الأُمّةَ المَفجوعةَ بصباح العَمَل
هذه العائلةَ التي تُعَلِّقُ صورةَ رأس المال في غرفة الجُلوس كأنّه
والدُها
اهْرُب مِنْ هذه الجزيرة
لا شيء وراءك سِوى الشّبابيك
شبابيك على مَدِّ النّظَر
شبابيك في النهار وشبابيك في الليل
واجهاتٌ مطفأة لآلامٍ مضاءة
واجهاتٌ مضيئةٌ لآلامٍ مطفأة
وتسمعُ الصوت: اهْرُب
بجميع لُغاتِ سُكّان المدينة الهاربين مِنْ أحلام طفولاتِهم
مِنْ آلامٍ مُستعمَراتٍ تحوّلت تواقيعَ باردةً في كتبٍ ماتَ مؤلِّفوها.
أولئك الهاربون ونَسَوا مِمّا هَربوا، الذين يَجبنون عن قَطْعِ الشارع

Escape

I hear a voice addressing me: *Escape —*
leave the English island behind you
you belong to nothing but this knock-off radio
nothing but the coffee-pot
nothing but the garden's trees outlined against a silken sky...
And I hear voices speak in languages that I know
and in languages that I do not know:
Escape —
leave behind you the clapped-out red buses,
the rusty train tracks,
this nation obsessed with morning work,
this family which hangs a picture of capitalism in the living
    room as if it were an ancestor —
escape from this island!
There are only windows behind you:
windows as far as you can see —
daylight windows,
nighttime windows,
dull facades for bright pains
bright facades for dull pains...
And you hear the voices:
Escape!
In every language of the city, from those still fleeing their
    childhood dreams,
from the pain of colonies that turn to cold signatures as their
    authors die —
the escapees who have forgotten what they escaped, too
    cowardly now to cross the street,

يَسْتَجمِعون الآن جُبْنهم ويَصرخون:
اهُرُب.

they gather all their cowardice together and scream:
Escape!

أمطار كوروساوا

الضَّجَرُ أَفْدَحُ مِنْ فَسادِ الطَّبيعَةِ البَشَرِيَّة
فَكَّرْتُ بهذا، وسَرَحَ خَيالي مَعَ كوروساوا
حينَما صَوَّر «المَلِك لير» وجَعَلَهُ يابانيّاً.

كانت هُناك أمطارٌ غَزيرةٌ
وكوروساوا يَسْتَوْرِدُ الغَضَبَ مِنْ لُغةٍ أُخرى
ولير يَهْذي باليابانيّة
أمَّا أنا فمِنْ أَجْلِ أَنْ يَتَكَلَّمَ بالعَرَبِيَّة رَبَّيتُ بناتي الثَّلاث في الخِزانة
ودرَّبْتُهُنَّ طَويلاً على الأدوار

الضَّجَرُ وفَسادُ الطَّبيعةِ البَشَريَّة
وَصَلا معاً على بَغْلةٍ واحِدة.

سأَعودُ إلى زِنْزانَةِ الفَنِّ الانْفِراديَّة
وأُغْلِقُ وَرائيَ الباب.

The Rain of Kurosawa

Boredom is worse than the corruption of human nature.
Thinking about this
my imagination zoomed in on Kurosawa
when he portrayed King Lear and made him Japanese.

In torrential rain
Kurosawa imports rage from another language:
Lear rants in Japanese.
And I, to let Lear speak Arabic, have raised my daughters
    in a cupboard
and trained them constantly on their roles.

Boredom and the corruption of human nature
arrived together on one mule.

I will retreat into art's solitary cell
and close the door.

ملاحَظة في الفَنّ الشِّعري

هناكَ شيءٌ مُشتَرَكٌ بَيْنَ جَميعِ أعدائي؛
كانوا قَبيحين.

وكُنْتُ أَعْرِفُ...
جميعُ القبيحينَ سَيَكونونَ أعدائي.

القبيحونَ
كانوا
جميعَ أعدائي.

A Note on the Art of Poetry

There was one thing all my enemies had in common:
they were ugly.

I just knew
all the ugly ones would be my enemies.

The ugly ones
were
all my enemies.

وجهُ صديق

إلى جون برجر

وَجْهُ صَديقٍ على رَفِّ «تاريخ الفَنّ»
في مَكْتَبَةٍ غَريبَة
وَجْهُ صَديقٍ مِنْ أَيّامِ بُيوتٍ مِنْ حَجَر
مِنْ أَيّامِ صَيْفِ القُرى
مِنْ تِلْكَ الأَرْضِ التي قَطَعَتْ وَريدَكَ مُنْذُ زَمَنٍ لَمْ تَعُدْ تَتَذَكَّرُه
تِلْكَ الأَرْضُ التي دَفَنَتْكَ وبَعَثَتْكَ مِراراً
وأحياناً كانت تَدْفِنُكَ ولا تَبْعَثُك
وأحياناً كُنْتَ تَتَوَسَّلُ إلِها أَنْ تَدْفِنَك

ما هو تاريخُ الفَنِّ أَصلاً إنْ لَمْ يَكُنْ وَجْهَ صديق؟

The Face of a Friend
for John Berger

The face of a friend on a shelf of art history books
in a strange library —
The face of a friend from days when the house was made of
  stone
from days when the village was made of summer
from land that cut you off at the wrist
in a time you no longer remember —
Land that buried you and resurrected you
  buried you and resurrected you
and sometimes it buried you without resurrecting you
and sometimes you begged it to bury you…

What is the history of art if not the face of a friend?

إلّا هذا الكأس

I

هذا البُرْجُ الذي يَرفُضُ أَنْ يَنْهار
رَغْمَ أَنَّ كُلَّ بُلْدوزَرات الدُّنيا تَضْرِبُ في أَساسِهِ
هَذه الأَيْقونةُ التي تَظَلُّ ناصِعَةً على حائطٍ عالٍ
رَغْمَ تَراشُقِ الوَحْل
رَغْمَ الحَضيضِ الذي يَلحَقُ بأَخيهِ الحَضيض
هذا الحُبُّ الذي يَرفُضُ أَنْ يَنْتَهي
رَغْمَ أَنَّ أَصحابَهُ انْتَهوا

يا ربّ، أَيَّ كأْسٍ تُريد
أَجرَعُهُ
لكِنْ أَجِزْ عَنّي بِلادي.

II

يا ربّ، إنَّ كُلَّ شيءٍ يَهْرَم
إلّا الشَّقاء يُجَدِّد شَبابَهُ
يا ربّ، إنَّ كُلَّ شيءٍ يَموت
إلّا المَأْساة
لا تَنْفَكُّ تُولَدُ عَذْراءَ مِنْ زَبَدِ هذا البَحْرِ الضَّائع...
يا ربّ، إنَّ كُلَّ شيءٍ يَنْهار
سِوى هذا الأَسى يَشُجُّ بابي
بِقَبْضَتين مَقْتولَتَين.

Except this Cup

I

This tower which refuses to collapse
despite all the bulldozers of the world striking its foundation,
this icon which remains radiant on its high wall
despite the splashing of mud,
despite abyss after abyss,
this love which refuses to end
even though we are done for.

Lord, from whichever cup you want me to drink
I would drink,
but not from my country's cup.

II

Everything grows old
except
misery renews its youth.

Everything dies
except
tragedy reborn as a virgin
from the foam of this lost sea…

Lord, everything collapses
except
this sorrow keeps knocking at my door
with dead hands.

أتعذّب بسعادتي

حينَ تَهْبِطُ عَلَيْكَ مائدَةٌ مِنَ المَنِّ والسَّلوى
وأباريقُ لَمْ تَرَ مِثلَها مِنْ خُمور الآلِهَة
ولا تَجِدُ أَحَداً سِوى نَفسِك
واقِفاً كالمُؤبِّن على رأسِ المَائِدَة
شُعورُكَ مِثلَ شُعوريَ الآنَ في زِنْزانَةِ السَّعادةِ الانْفِراديَّة
عِنْدي بَحْرٌ وجَبَل
والذينَ أُحِبُّهم في المَنفى.

40

Pained by Happiness

When a feast from heaven descends
with jugs full of the wine of the gods
and you find no one but yourself
standing like a eulogist at the head of the table —
then you will feel as I do now in the solitary cell of happiness:
I have a sea and a mountain
while my loved ones are in exile.

دفتر

تُضَيِّعُهُ يَومَين فَتَضيعُ حَياتُك
تَعثُرُ عَلَيْهِ فَتَجِدُها مِنْ جَديد
خَفيفَةً
وهَشَّةً
وما مِنْ سارِقٍ
إلّا ويَطلُبُها.

The Notebook

You lose the notebook for two days, and then you lose your life.
You find the notebook, and then your life is found anew —
light,
delicate,
there is no thief
who does not covet it.

اللّصوص

اللُّصوصُ كانوا يَسْرِقونَ أَغْناماً وذَهَباً
سَمِعْتُ عَنْ واحِدٍ سَرَقوا زَوْجَتَه
وكُثُرٌ سُرِقَتْ مَحافِظُهُم وسَيّاراتُهُم
لَكِنْ مَنْ يُصَدِّقُني حينَ أَقولُ إنَّ بِلادي
بِجِبالِها وبَحْرِها
بِسَمائِها الزَّرْقاء
بِقُرىً سَكَنَها اللهُ واحِدَةً واحِدَة
مَنْ يُصَدِّقُني
حينَ أَقولُ إنَّها سُرِقَتْ.

The Thieves

The thieves used to steal sheep and gold —
I heard about one man, they stole his wife —
and others whose wallets and cars were stolen,
but who would believe me when I say that my country
with its mountains and sea
its blue sky
and its villages that God has visited one by one,
who believes me
when I say that they have been stolen?

عن طفولتي

... ولم أَكُنْ أَسْأَلُ عَن طُفولَتي
ولا أخبارِ المَحْكَمَة
هناك حَيْثُ رَفَعْنا مَرَّةً دَعوى
ضِدَّ الذينَ سَرَقوها.

About My Childhood

I did not ask about my childhood
or about the court's verdict
after we had presented our case
against those who stole it.

ثلاثون سنة إلى الوراء

أُريدُ أَنْ تُعيدَني هَذِهِ الكَلِماتُ ثَلاثينَ سَنَةً إلى الوَراء
حَيْثُ أَشجارٌ لَمْ تُقطَعْ ووديانٌ لَمْ تُجرَف
وزَيْتونٌ
ورُمَّانٌ
ومُسْتَقْبَلٌ يَتَلَثَّمُ بِكوفِيَّةِ المَاضي.

بِلادٌ تَتَنَقَّلُ كالجُندول بين الكابوس والحُلم...

أَيَسْتَطيعُ هؤلاء الغُزاةُ أَنْ يَسْرِقوا المَاضي
الذي كانَ هوَ المُسْتَقْبَل؟

Thirty Years Back

I want words to take me thirty years back
before the trees were cut, before the valleys were ploughed.
There were olives
and pomegranates
and a future masked with a kuffiyyah of the past,

a country sliding like a gondola between nightmare and dream.

Can those invaders steal the past that was the future?

هاوية شعبي

لا يُمْكِنُكَ أَنْ تَقولَ عَنْ شَعْبِيَ شيئاً لا أَعْرِفُه
فَكَما انْحَدَرْتُ مِنْ سَمائِهِ وغَيمِهِ وجبالِه
فإنَّني أَيضاً خَبِرْتُ سُفوحَهُ وكُهوفَهُ المُظْلِمَة
وعِنْدي نُسْخةٌ كامِلةٌ مِنْ دفترِ موبِقاتِه
حَتَّى ضِباعُهُ وأَفاعيه
أَحدِبُ عَلَيْها وأُحِبُّها.

لقد طوَّحَ بِيَ الشَّكُّ كثيراً في إلـهي
لكنّي لَمْ أَشُكَّ بِهِ مَرَّةً واحِدة
وإليهِ نَسَبْتُ كُلَّ ما يَسْتَحِقُّ الحياة
لَيْسَ حُبّي لهُ وَحْدَهُ الأَعمى
أنا أَيضاً أَعمى
أَسْلَمْتُ لهُ قِيادي
وأعْرِفُ أَنَّهُ يَسيرُ بي إلى الهاوية.

My People's Abyss

You cannot say anything about my people that I do not
    already know.
For I am descended from their sky, clouds and mountains,
I have mastered their dark caves,
and have a full tally of their sins —
their hyenas and snakes
even these I care for and love.

I often have my doubts about God
but I have never doubted my people.
All that deserves to live, I attribute to them.
It is not only my love for them that is blind:
I am also blind.
I have given them my hand,
and I know they are leading me towards the abyss.

حتّى السماء

جِبالٌ تَتَهاوى في رأسي
مُروجٌ مَبْلولةٌ تَنْزَلِقُ واحِداً وَراءَ آخَر
حَتَّى السَّماء
الواحِدةُ فَوْقَ كُلِّ النّاس
لَمْ تَعُدْ سَمائي.

Even the Sky

Mountains collapsing in my head,
dew-wet meadows, slipping one after another,
even the sky —
the only one all people share —
is no longer my sky.

أنا شبحٌ وأعرف عمّا أتحدّث

خَطَرَ لي
بَيْنَما الأَمطارُ تَسَاقَطُ فَوقَ أَشجارٍ آسيَويَّةٍ
أَسْفَلَ سُورِ الصّين
بَيْنَما نَحْنُ هُناك نَشْرُبُ الشّاي
ونُنْصِتُ ناعِسِينَ لِقَصائدِ بَعْضِنا
خَطَرَ لي أَن أَقولَ لَهُم:
نَحْنُ أَشْباحٌ هاهُنا.

تَتَجَمَّعُ الأَشْباحُ لِتَتَدَفَّأ
تَسيرُ في جَماعاتٍ
لأنَّها تَعْرِفُ أَنَّها لَيْسَت مِنَ الجَماعَة
أَنا شَبَحٌ وأَعْرِفُ عَمَّا أَتَحَدّث

خَطَرَ لي وكَتَمتُ الخاطِر
فالأَشْباحُ تَعْرِفُ هذا
ولا تُحِبُّ أَن تَسْمَعَهُ مِن أَحَد
الأَشْباحُ تُحاوِلُ أَن تَنْسى
وحينَ تَلْتَقي في جَماعاتٍ
فهيَ تَلْتَقي لِتَنْسى
تَشْرَبُ الشّاي
وتَقْرَأُ القَصائدَ على مَسامِعِ بَعْضِها
لِتَنْسى.

نَحْنُ الآن
أَسْفَلَ سُورِ الصّين
والأَمطارُ تَسَاقَطُ
الشّاي يوشِكُ أَن يَنْتَهي
وكذلك القَصائدُ
أَنا شَبَحٌ وأَعْرِفُ عَمَّا أَتَحَدّث.

54

I am a Ghost and I Know what I'm Talking About

It occurred to me
as rain was falling on the trees
by the Great Wall of China
where we were drinking tea
and listening sleepily to each other's poems,
it occurred to me to tell them:
We are ghosts here.

Ghosts gather together to keep warm,
they walk in groups
for they know they don't belong.
I am a ghost and I know what I'm talking about.

It occurred to me but I suppressed the thought:
ghosts know this already,
they do not like to hear anyone speak of it,
ghosts try to forget
and when they meet in groups
they meet to forget —
they drink tea
and recite poems to each other
to forget.

We are here now
by the Great Wall of China:
rain is falling
and our tea is about to end —
the poems as well.
I am a ghost and I know what I'm talking about.

Afterword

The 16th century French essayist, Michel de Montaigne, said that when reason isn't enough, experience may lead us to knowledge. Poetry is the experience of someone else's experience, the experience of their language. Reading Najwan Darwish's poems in these fine translations, I am drawn to the uncanny nature of this experience. There is an effusive rawness in the way he writes, yet the poems are always exquisitely constructed. They are shockingly immediate and yet seem premeditated. They are truthful to their settings, often historically identifiable events, but seem to resonate beyond any one-dimensional context. Darwish's poetry opens up for me a world not entirely familiar; yet it translates into my consciousness. Darwish and I may inhabit different times – because lived time is heterogeneous, despite the universal calendar and clock time ordained by modernity and Western colonialism – but we both inhabit an existential space that colonialism has failed to overwhelm: the diverse narratives of our cultural experience. I read Darwish's poetry through a position we share in our anticolonial struggle, a position marked by loss, estrangement and political cruelty. His poetry bears witness to this paradoxical experience: the assault on culture and the resistance of the imagination.

Darwish is a master of turning a private utterance into a universal claim. Take the opening poem, for instance. See how much he achieves with a small twist to a line by the 10th century Arab philosopher, al-Ma'arri:

My body is a blue the sky has long forgotten;
my body is a garden lost to the spring.
You, 'tailor of the universe',
what would be lost by not sewing me?

Al-Ma'arri was blind, yet here he inspires a poem on the intensity of vision, when the gaze is turned inwards. The limitations of the body, of outward experience, can open up an infinite interiority.

To be blind may be an accident of fate, but to be a refugee is an accident of historical design. In the very next poem, 'In Front of a Church in the Settlement of Antigua', we find another layer of Darwish's poetic identity – his empathy across cultures. Here the speaker of the poem encounters the statue of the Virgin Mary, a peasant girl from Palestine, who tells the poet her story. The statue of the peasant girl comes alive in the poem, no longer bound by the rigid state of her iconography. The association between the poet and the statue belongs to a cultural history that has been fenced off by modern, Western narratives of identity. It is a poet's task to overcome the false cleavages of history. All too often these political determinations congeal into fate, but in Darwish's poetry the imagination has a liberating force: the impossible becomes possible.

That said, Darwish's poetry is often heartbreakingly pessimistic even in its moments of transcendence. In the title poem, 'Embrace', the poet embraces nothingness. The poem hallucinates another contradictory, impossible state:

Confused, wet through,
my corpse also stretches out its arms,
clutching, to embrace the sea that drowns it.

The poet's relationship with his homeland has passed into a natural state of life stripped bare. An attempt to reconcile this alienation evokes a delirious death wish.

This sense of entrapment in the fate of larger discourses is explored further in 'Words at the Gate of Jerusalem'. Here the speaker of the poem is circumscribed by the intensity of his devotion: 'My Lord, the Prophet chained me between Jerusalem and Mecca: / I cannot leave the space between them.

/ I am waiting for him'. Jerusalem and Mecca are like two eyes, and the poet knits his brow in the space between them. It is marked by a time of erasures and exile. But most particularly, it is the loss of language that gives the poem its stake and intensity: 'For what are Mecca and Jerusalem without their language?'

This centrality of language – the problem, and potential, of expression itself – is a recurrent concern for Darwish. The German poet, Friedrich Hölderlin, raised the question: '…and what are poets for in a destitute time?' and Darwish's poems are an urgent response to that question. The poems are a bridge between the long 20th century and the 21st. The world has undergone spectacular changes. But as Darwish reminds us, in poem after poem, what agonizingly persists is the exiled state of our being and language. It is a realisation made possible for us, his English readers, because of the excellence of his translators. Atef Alshaer and Paul Batchelor's translations achieve a fine balance between the evocative quality of the poems and their terse intensity. The poem, 'At a Poetry Festival', is a characteristically taut tightrope between the poles of directness and irony. The wry colloquial manner of the voice and the sense of desolation is judged to perfection in the English. The emphasis is kept off the language so the shock of the unexpected last word is all the more effective: 'It neither arrives nor returns. / It neither arrives nor drowns'.

Darwish is acutely aware of the risks of translation and animates them with great wit in the poem 'The Rain of Kurosawa'. Here he muses: 'I, to let Lear speak Arabic, have raised my daughters in a cupboard / and trained them constantly on their roles.' The imagination is comic, at once serious and amusing: the desire for corruption is translatable from culture to culture. But it mockingly alludes to the cultural presumptions, whether these are actual or perceived is left to the reader's judgement.

This ironic uncertainty is also deployed in the poem, 'My People's Abyss', Darwish writes: 'You cannot say anything about my people that I do not already know.' This is not the objective claim of the historian or sociologist, it is a poetic claim – at once more intimate and more ironic.

> I have mastered their dark caves,
> and have a full tally of their sins —
> their hyenas and snakes
> even these I care for and love.

Belonging comes with a price. So does love. Darwish intensifies the irony as he ends the poem: 'I have given them my hand, / and I know they are leading me towards the abyss.' The abyss to which he is being led is a black hole of possibilities. The speaker can *belong* to his people – he can't *be* his people. It is hazardous to look for lost origins in the wreckage of the present. The abyss can signify the origin as much as the endpoint.

In 'Except this Cup', Darwish begins: 'This tower which refuses to collapse / despite all the bulldozers of the world striking its foundation'. It reminds me of what the French writer, Christian Salmon, wrote in *Le Monde Diplomatique* in 2002, after he visited Palestine along with other writers, to meet Mahmoud Darwish in house arrest: "This is the first war to be waged with bulldozers... This is war in an age of agoraphobia, a fear of open spaces, seeking not the division of territory but its abolition.' The intention is clearly not just to destroy a material object, but to erase its memory, sever its ties with the land.

Darwish's own poetry seems to serve a double task: to keep hammering his words against the hammers that seek to destroy the signs of his civilisation, as well as to recount the unfinished horrors that refuse to pass from before his eyes. In the same poem, he writes:

Lord, everything collapses
except
this sorrow keeps knocking at my door
with dead hands.

Like sea waves crashing against the rocks, there is a relentless consistency of grief. Darwish speaks of a disembodied sorrow. It is the sorrow of the dead that pervades the agoraphobic air of the living.

Rarely does this sorrow find release. In 'The Face of a Friend', dedicated to John Berger, Darwish discovers, 'The face of a friend on a shelf of art history books / in a strange library'. It is a Borgesian moment of encounter, where the poet discovers the familiar in the midst of strangeness. He writes:

The face of a friend from days when the house was
        made of stone
from days when the village was made of summer
from land that cut you off at the wrist
in a time you no longer remember

This account of friendship is the recounting of time, often from different horizons. Darwish is a Palestinian poet from Jerusalem, who breathes the world. The face of Berger enters the poem like the frame of a window that helps the poet escape for a moment from the torn landscape of memory. It is a point of intersection between art and history.

In his famous speech, 'The Meridian', delivered on 22 October, 1960, Paul Celan imagined the poem as 'lonely and *en route*' and, from its inception, seeking 'the mystery of the encounter'. Celan evokes the metaphor of the 'meridian' to indicate a terrestrially imagined arc that passes from the poet to 'the figure of the other'. I read Darwish's poem for Berger as a similar attempt. The poem records an encounter between two different cultural worlds that understand each other through a language of art that is lost in history and politics. Berger evokes in Darwish another time lost to memory. The mutuality of friendship alone seems capable of recovering this lost time and the abiding mystery of meeting. The striking last line of the poem reads: 'What is the history of art if not the face of a friend?' Without the deeper relationships, the history of art is a depersonalized artefact of the past. It is cold, part of the shelf of an unfamiliar library. The position presented in the poem is anti-Platonic: art is not an abstract and objective idea. The history of art is the artist.

There is a strong wish to recover the past in Darwish's poetry. In 'Thirty Years Back' he writes, 'I want words to take me thirty years back / before the trees were cut, before the valleys were ploughed.' The time of destitution is countable. What can't be measured is the endless nightmare that followed the disfiguration of time. There is no paradise on earth, except a childhood that was destroyed by history. But Darwish's poetry does not simply evoke an Edenic past, it registers the impossibility of it. All that the poet can reclaim are shards from a memory that has been altered forever. The precarious image of the 'sliding gondola' takes us back to the image of the corpse drowning at sea in the poem, 'Embrace': be it the self or country, the ground of history has given way, and the poet encounters the whirlpool of experience. The poem ends enigmatically: 'Can those invaders steal the past that was the future?' What for Proust was simply the memory of the past, is for Darwish what cannot be stitched back into the future. For now, Darwish must bang the doors of the present and reclaim the past on paper.

We are back here to the question of experience, even if that is the experience of an absence. Darwish reminds us that poets can transcend their locations to experience the otherness of genuine encounter. This meeting with otherness, with what might have been, is paradoxical, a form of experiencing the unexperienceable. It is the real work of the imagination.

Darwish's poetry illuminates the dark zones that fall in the interstices between language and history. He is looking for signs of association, a foothold of familiarity, among the world's strangers.

Manash Firaq Bhattacharjee

Najwan Darwish is a Palestinian poet born in Jerusalem. He published his first book of poetry in 2000 and has been an important literary figure ever since. He has published eight books in Arabic, and his work has been translated into over twenty languages. New York Review Books, which published the English translation of his collection *Nothing More to Lose* in 2014, describes him as 'one of the foremost Arabic-language poets of his generation'.

Darwish has co-founded and directed cultural projects throughout the Arab world and served as the literary advisor to the Palestine Festival of Literature. He has held many key positions in cultural journalism and has been the Chief Cultural Editor of the Arabic-language London-based newspaper *Al Araby Al Jadeed* since 2014. Darwish lives between Jerusalem and Haifa.

Atef Alshaer is an academic, translator and poet. He is senior lecturer in Arabic Studies at the University of Westminster and is the author of several publications in the fields of language, literature and politics, including *Poetry and Politics in the Modern Arab World* (Hurst, 2016) and *A Map of Absence: An Anthology of Palestinian Writing on the Nakba* (Saqi, 2019).

Paul Batchelor is a poet born in Northumberland. He is the author of the pamphlet *To Photograph a Snow Crystal* (Smith/ Doorstop, 2006) and *The Sinking Road* (Bloodaxe, 2008). He has won the Times Stephen Spender Prize for Translation and the Edwin Morgan International Poetry Prize, and he writes criticism for the *Guardian* and the *TLS*.

Manash Firaq Bhattacharjee is a poet, writer, translator and political science scholar. He is the author of *The Town Slowly Empties: On Life and Culture during Lockdown* (Headpress, forthcoming), *Looking for the Nation: Towards Another Idea of India* (Speaking Tiger, 2018) and *Ghalib's Tomb and Other Poems* (The London Magazine, 2013).

About the Poetry Translation Centre

Set up in 2004, the Poetry Translation Centre is the only UK organisation dedicated to translating, publishing and promoting contemporary poetry from Africa, Asia and Latin America. We introduce extraordinary poets from around the world to new audiences through books, online resources and bilingual events. We champion diversity and representation in the arts, and forge enduring relations with diaspora communities in the UK. We explore the craft of translation through our long-running programme of workshops which are open to all.

The Poetry Translation Centre is based in London and is an Arts Council National Portfolio organisation. To find out more about us, including how you can support our work, please visit: www.poetrytranslation.org.

About the World Poet Series

The *World Poet Series* offers an introduction to some of the world's most exciting contemporary poets in an elegant pocket-sized format. The books are presented as bilingual editions, with the English and original-language text displayed side by side. The translations have emerged from specially commissioned collaborations between translators and English-language poets. Completing each book is an afterword essay by a poet responding to the translations.